# Standin' Tall® with DEPENDABILITY

Music by
**Janeen Brady**
Script by
**Diane Woolley** and **Janeen Brady**

**Series Includes**
1. Obedience
2. Honesty
3. Forgiveness
4. Work
5. Courage
6. Happiness
7. Gratitude
8. Love
9. Service
10. Cleanliness
11. Self-Esteem
★12. Dependability

©Copyright 1984 by Janeen Brady. All rights reserved. No part of this book may be reproduced in any form. Printed in the United States of America.

Reggie, Kate, you haven't returned your library books, and I was depending on you.

Kate: We'll take them back, Mom.

★ **In a minute.**

Why must you procrastinate?

KATE: Procrastinate?

★ **What's that?**

Waiting for a later time to do what you are supposed to do now.

KATE: But sometimes I don't like to do what I have to do. I'd rather do what I want to do.

Kate, when a job has to be done, putting it off only makes it harder.

★ **Oh, Mom, that's what you always say.**

Only because it's right, Reggie. Someday you'll learn how important dependability is.

Doing what you're taught to do, ought to do, got to do,
Doing what you promise to when you say you'll do it,
That's dependability; that's dependability.

D-E-P-E-N-dability helps you face responsibility.
D-E-P-E-N-dability shows that you're prepared.
D-E-P-E-N-dability lends to your respectability.
Everyone should, everyone could, be dependable.

Being where you say you'll be, on the dot, punctually,
Never late, not you, not me, that's all there is to it.
That's dependability, that's dependability.

(Chorus)

★ **I guess we should try to be more dependable, even though I don't see what all the fuss is about. I don't think dependability is that important.**

KATE: Reggie, I don't think you should have said that.

★ **What's going on? Where are we?**

KATE: Don't look now, but I think we're in a space ship in outer space—and we're not alone.

SPACEWOMAN: Captain Dependable, we're being invaded. Professor Un and his awful henchmen are everywhere. They're trying to take command of our ship, sir.

CAPTAIN DEPENDABLE: So, the wicked Professor Un has found us. Secure the air locks. Alarm systems to Code 10. Nothing to worry about, crew, this is Captain Dependable, and everything is under control.

I'm Captain Dependable; you can always count on me.
I'm Captain Dependable; I come through, as you will see.
Should someone need me, never fear,
Almost like magic I'll appear.
I'm not just intendable—Captain Dependable, that's me.

CAPTAIN DEPENDABLE: First we must see to Prince Reginald and Princess Katrina's safety.

KATE: He thinks we're a prince and princess.

CAPTAIN DEPENDABLE: Your Highnesses, we must hide you.

SPACEWOMAN: Sir, enemy forces have broken through our security. They're entering through cargo gate four.

CAPTAIN DEPENDABLE: To your stations! I'll get the prince and princess below to safety. They must not fall into Professor Un's hands. Hurry, Your Majesties, this way.

PROFESSOR UN: Ha! ha! ha! ha! Set your stun guns, men. I shall have control of this ship immediately. Find the prince and princess and Captain Dependable. I have plans for him. And hurry!

HENCHMAN: But, Professor Un, Captain Dependable, he'll—

PROFESSOR UN: Ha, Captain Dependable! You need fear him no longer. I have prepared a little treat for the great Captain Dependable. Bring me the box.

HENCHMAN: What's in it?

PROFESSOR UN: You ask what's in it? I'll tell you what's in it. Procrastinite!

HENCHMAN: Procrastinite! Professor Un, you're a genius.

PROFESSOR UN: Yes, I know, and this shall be the undoing of our dear Captain Dependable. When he is near procrastinite, it will make him put off what he is supposed to do. He will procrastinate!

CAPTAIN DEPENDABLE: Prince Reginald, Princess Katrina, you will be safe in here. I'll just actuate the magnetic seal here on the door, and no one will be able to enter. You're in good hands with Captain Dependable.

PROFESSOR UN: There he is! Quick, men, open the box.

CAPTAIN DEPENDABLE: What's happening? Everything is slowing down. Suddenly I don't feel like doing anything. Everything can just wait.

KATE: Seal the door, Captain Dependable.

CAPTAIN DEPENDABLE: In a minute. I'm going to get a bite to eat.

★ **Captain Dependable, we need you—now!**

CAPTAIN DEPENDABLE: I'll be right back.

PROFESSOR UN: Did you see that? He's ruined forever. Dependable, ha! And now, my good captain, the UN-FUN has begun.

Hooray, Professor Un!
Touché, Professor Un!
Your secret weapon cast its spell
On Captain (ha!) Dependable.
The dread procrastinite
Has overcome his might.
His friends he'll nevermore defend.
On such as he they can't depend.
Hurray, Professor Un!
Touché, Professor Un!
Hurray, Professor Un!
The UN-FUN has begun,
Begun, begun.

PROFESSOR UN: Now to find the prince and the princess.

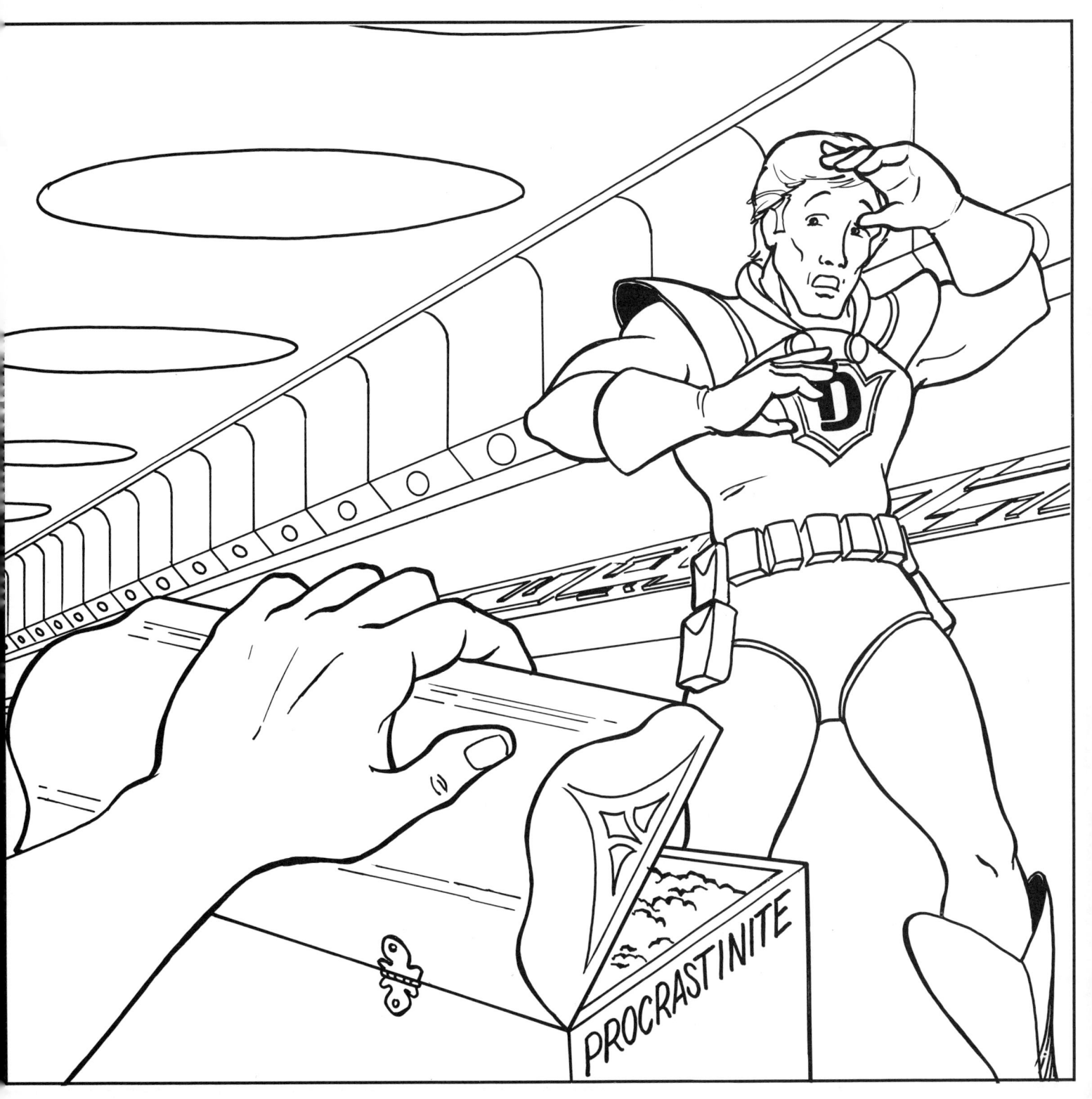

KATE: I've locked the door from the inside. That will delay them for a few moments.

★ Quick! We've got to find someplace to hide.

KATE: What's that up there?

★ It's an air vent. Do you think it's big enough to hold us?

KATE: Looks like our only chance. Boost me up. Got it!

★ Climb in, grab my wrists, and pull me up. I'm in—barely in time.

HENCHMAN: They're gone—not here anywhere.

PROFESSOR UN: Find them! Search everywhere. There may be an escape hatch we don't know about.

HENCHMAN: We'll get them for you, Professor.

HENCHMAN II: The ship's control base has been secured, Professor Un.

PROFESSOR UN: Splendid! Get the procrastinite and carry it carefully to the control room. Leave the lid open; it will make anyone who comes near it undependable.

KATE: They're gone.

★ For now. Somebody has to do something about Professor Un. Quiet, I hear footsteps.

CAPTAIN DEPENDABLE: (Humming.)

★ Captain Dependable, help us down.

CAPTAIN DEPENDABLE: Oh, Prince Reginald, Princess Katrina, what are you doing up there?

KATE: You didn't seal the door like you said you would, remember?

CAPTAIN DEPENDABLE: Oh, my! I got involved. But it was a delicious sandwich. Lots of mustard and a pickle and—

★ Good grief, Captain, will you please help us down?

CAPTAIN DEPENDABLE: Well, I guess. Hey, is that a TV? I wonder what's on.

KATE: Captain, we must make plans.

CAPTAIN DEPENDABLE: Look, my favorite show. We can plan as soon as it gets to a commercial.

★ **But we need your help now.**

♪♪ In a minute, in a while, I will do it with a smile.
Just a second, I'll get to it.
When the commercial comes, I'll jump right up and do it.
Not right now; I'm too tired. But tomorrow I'll be inspired.
Then I'll do it, never fear it.
That sounds easy, 'cause tomorrow isn't here yet.

Later, wait till later, I will get it done just the way you say.
Later, wait till later, but don't make me do it today.
I don't want to. I feel dizzy. Do I have to? I'm so busy.
It's upsetting when you scold me.
And I promise you I'll do it like you told me. Later!

KATE: Oh, Prince Reginald, it's so sad. He was so dependable.

★ **And look at him now. He'll never get anything accomplished again.**

CAPTAIN DEPENDABLE: That's right. I shall start projects and never finish them. I'll tell people I'll do things and then not do them. I'll put off cleaning my room and picking up after myself until this ship will look like a pig pen. Oh, I'm brokenhearted! Professor Un has UNDEPENDABILIZED me.

KATE: Isn't there anything we can do? Think, Captain—uh—Dependable.

CAPTAIN DEPENDABLE: I don't know. Wait! There is something. My DO-IT-NOW wafers! They're hidden in a secret compartment on the outside of the ship between the sixth and seventh rocket boosters.

★ **Wonderful! Let's go get them. You'll have to show us the way.**

CAPTAIN DEPENDABLE: I can hardly wait to be dependable again. We'll do it first thing tomorrow.

★ **Tomorrow?**

CAPTAIN DEPENDABLE: Sure! It can wait.

KATE: But it will be too late. Professor Un will capture us.

CAPTAIN DEPENDABLE: Oh, I doubt it's that urgent.

★ **Princess Katrina, we're going to have to do this ourselves. When someone is undependable, that's all you can do.**

KATE: It's awful when you depend on someone and they don't come through. Oh, no!

PROFESSOR UN: Aha! The prince and princess! Seize them!

★ **Professor Un has seen us. Run! Here, into this air-lock chamber!**

KATE: Look! Space suits! Let's put them on, and maybe we can find the DO-IT-NOW wafers ourselves.

★ **Princess Katrina, look at all the stars.**

KATE: I'd rather not, thank you. I'll just hold tight to my life line.

★ **Where did Captain Dependable say the secret compartment was?**

KATE: Between the sixth and seventh boosters.

★ **This is number five. Six is right here.**

PROFESSOR UN: Ha! ha! ha!

KATE: Oh, no, there's Professor Un.

PROFESSOR UN: Now I have you. I think the worst fate for you, my little friends, is to untie your life lines. I'll let you float into the next galaxy. That should keep you busy for a while. Eh!

KATE: Oh, no, please don't. Help! Help!

★ **We're drifting away from the space ship.**

♪ Hooray, Professor Un!
Touché, Professor Un!
He's sent off to a fate untold
Katrina and Prince Reginald.
The ship's in our command.
The captain's in our hands.
We'll fly through space, Professor Un
And nothing ever will get done.
Hooray, Professor Un!
The captain is UN-done.
Hooray, Professor Un!
The captain is UN-done,
UN-done, UN-done.

KATE: Captain Dependable, throw us a life line.

CAPTAIN DEPENDABLE: Just a minute! I'm talking with a friend.

★ **Captain—be dependable!**

KATE: We're doomed unless we think of something quick.

★ **It's too bad we didn't bring a rocket booster.**

KATE: Prince Reginald, that's it! We're wearing Captain Dependable's space suits, and they always have . . .

★ **. . . a built-in, compact, computerized, self-propelling rocket booster. Here it is!**

KATE: It's so tiny! Do you think it will get us both back to the ship?

★ **It's our only chance. Hang on tight and let's give it a try.**

KATE: It worked!

★ **Now let's rescue Captain Dependable.**

KATE: How are we going to do that—magic?

★ **No, brains. There's the secret compartment. Open it.**

KATE: Here they are, Captain Dependable's DO-IT-NOW wafers.

★ **Now let's get back through the escape hatch, Princess.**

KATE: That procrastinite seems to have affected more than Captain Dependable. Nobody's doing what they're supposed to. This space ship is a mess.

★ **It's a good thing our chemical makeup is different from this crew's. The procrastinite doesn't affect us.**

CAPTAIN DEPENDABLE: Princess Katrina, how did you get back here?

KATE: Captain Dependable, am I glad to see you! Here, eat this.

CAPTAIN DEPENDABLE: Okay, as soon as I get around to it.

KATE: No, eat it now!

CAPTAIN DEPENDABLE: All right, if I have to. Oh, my, that tastes very much like a DO-IT-NOW wafer. It is! I can feel it!

I'm Captain Dependable!
You can always count on me.
I'm Captain Dependable. I come through, as you will see.
Should someone need me, never fear,
Almost like magic I'll appear.
I'm not just intendable—Captain Dependable, that's me!

CAPTAIN DEPENDABLE: Where's a life line? Someone called for a life line.

★ **That's already been taken care of, Captain.**

CAPTAIN DEPENDABLE: There must be something that needs to be done.

KATE: Sh! Here comes Professor Un. Don't let him see us.

PROFESSOR UN: What a disgusting mess this ship is—things out of place, work undone, we're off course. Oh, I love it!

CAPTAIN DEPENDABLE: Not so fast, Professor Un.

PROFESSOR UN: Captain Dependable!

CAPTAIN DEPENDABLE: With emphasis on the "DEPENDABLE." Take your Un-dependable crew and leave this ship immediately. Dependability triumphs again!

★ **Before that DO-IT-NOW wafer wears off, Captain, I'm going to get rid of this procrastinite.**

KATE: Let's put it in a rocket booster and send it to the deepest, darkest part of the galaxy. Three, two, one, fire!

CAPTAIN DEPENDABLE: And now, Prince Reginald and Princess Katrina, I present you this ship's highest award for dependability above and beyond the call of duty.

You were where you said you'd be. You get a hundred in dependability.
You did what you said you'd do. You're dependable through and through.
You were prompt. You came on time.
Being dependable's a habit of mine.
You can put your trust in me.
You get a hundred.
I get a hundred.
You get a hundred in dependability.

I was where I said I'd be. I get a hundred in dependability.
I did what I said I'd do. I'm dependable through and through.
I was prompt. I came on time. Being dependable's a habit of mine.
You can put your trust in me.
I get a hundred,
I get a hundred in dependability.

KATE: Reggie, we're back! We're home again!

★ **Mom, you wouldn't believe where we've been.**

Weren't you saying something about dependability being unimportant?

★ **Don't say it, Mom. Don't even think it.**

KATE: We've changed. From now on you'll be amazed how dependable we'll be—better than the captain himself.

★ **Come on, Kate, let's take these books back.**

Now, remember . . .

Straight home, straight aim, straight arrow.
I'm depending on, I'm depending on you.
Straight home, straight aim, straight arrow.
Are you following, are you following through?

Straight home, don't hang around the neighborhood.
Straight aim, just do your best; you know you should.
Straight arrow, stay far away from what's not good.
Then, when you're away, I'll know you're okay.

Straight home, straight aim, straight arrow.
I'm depending on, I'm depending on you.
Straight home, straight aim, straight arrow.
Are you following, are you following through?

**Side A** of each cassette contains the complete program. **Side B** repeats the same program but leaves out the lines of the main child in the story, giving the listener the chance to read along, saying aloud the missing lines and actually becoming a member of the cast. This fascinating activity helps older children with their reading and provides an excellent opportunity for development in dramatics.

Children can sing along with the songs, color the pictures and participate in still other activities as the story progresses.

A Product of BRITE MUSIC ENTERPRISES, INC.

Music and Dramatics recorded, engineered and mixed at Bonneville Media Communications.
Illustrations by Neil Galloway / Graphic production by Whipple & Associates.
Music arranged and conducted by Merrill Jenson.